MEET THE WOMEN OF

American
Soccer

An Inside Look at America's Team

MEET THE WOMEN OF

American Soccer

An Inside Look at America's Team

by Wayne Coffey
photographs by Michael Stahlschmidt

SCHOLASTIC INC.
New York   Toronto   London   Auckland   Sydney
Mexico City   New Delhi   Hong Kong

**"Thanks to all of our families
for giving us the courage to believe
and the strength to succeed."**
—members of the U.S. Women's National Team

Ed Purcell/Meridian Images

MEET THE PHOTOGRAPHER

All of the photographs in this book were taken by Michael Stahlschmidt, one of America's best and busiest sports photographers.

Stahlschmidt, who owns Sideline Sports Photography in Lake Forest, Illinois, has shot photographs for hundreds of publications and soccer organizations around the world, among them Nike, adidas, Reebok, *Newsweek*, *Sports Illustrated*, FIFA, and US Soccer. His many assignments have included photographing World Cup USA 1994, Women's World Cup Sweden 1995, the 1996 Atlanta Olympics, the 1998 World Cup in France, and he is currently Director of Photography for the MLS Champion Chicago Fire.

ISBN 0-439-08654-X

© 1999 by All-American Soccer Stars.
All team photos: Michael Stahlschmidt/SSP © 1999
All rights reserved. Published by Scholastic Inc.

12 11 10 9 8 7 6 5 4 3 2 1   9/9 0 1 2 3 4/0

Printed in the U.S.A.
First Scholastic printing, May 1999
Book design: Michael Malone

Carla and Julie at the White House.

Dear Fan,

Welcome to an inside look at our team. We hope you enjoy reading about our fun, wacky, dedicated teammates as much as we enjoy playing with them. While there are many ingredients that contribute to success on the field, we believe the strength of our team is rooted in our unity.

We not only play soccer together every day, but we also live together in residency, travel together, eat together, shop together…basically, we spend A LOT of time together! And with three children traveling with us around the world (Joy Fawcett's kids, Katey and Carli; and Carla Overbeck's son, Jackson), we truly redefine the term "family." A BIG family. Thank goodness we all get along so well!!!

So welcome to our wonderful world of soccer, friendship, family, and complete dedication to a team and sport we all love. We hope you will become a part of our family as we attempt to recapture the World Cup trophy this summer in the Women's World Cup, right here in the United States. Then it's off to Sydney, Australia, to defend our gold medal in the 2000 Summer Olympics. Thanks for your support over the years—every single one of you has made a difference!

Sincerely,

Carla Overbeck
#4
Carla Overbeck

Julie Foudy
#11
Julie Foudy

This is the team...Now is the time.

It is a few minutes after eight o'clock on a hot humid night in Athens, Georgia. The first women's soccer gold-medal game in Olympic history is about to begin. Every seat in the University of Georgia's Sanford Stadium is filled.

Tiffeny Milbrett; Shannon MacMillan

While the teams from the U.S. and China trot onto the field, the American players can't help but look up toward the lights and the upper reaches of the stadium. The fans give them a roaring welcome. Flashbulbs go off by the thousands. The attendance will later be announced as 76,489—the largest crowd in history to witness a women's sporting event. For the veterans of the U.S. team, it is impossible not to think of the days, not long ago, when the team's fans could be counted on fingers and toes.

"People didn't know women even played soccer," star U.S. midfielder Kristine Lilly says. "You'd tell them, 'I play for the U.S. National Team,' and they'd say, 'What's that?'"

1996 Olympic team

Nearly three years after that historic moment, the U.S. National Team is gearing up for another one. This summer, for the first time, the United States is hosting the Women's World Cup—the most important women's soccer competition since the Olympics.

The event will feature the top sixteen teams in the world, playing a total of thirty-two games. It will start June 19 and run to July 10, the date of the World Cup final, at the Rose Bowl in Pasadena, California. With every game televised and large crowds expected from coast to coast, it is being hailed as the biggest women's sporting event in history.

The players of the U.S. National Team know exactly what they're getting into. And they can't wait. But perhaps what makes them most excited of all is that the 1999 World Cup will be one more chance to renew the special bond they have with their fans.

"Our fans are amazing," U.S. co-captain Julie Foudy says.

"I've always felt we have the best fans in the world," says Mia Hamm, the team's record-setting forward and the most well-known female soccer player in the world. "And this is our chance to showcase that."

The U.S. women may have a connection with their supporters that is unmatched in any national team sport. To know it, all you need to do is attend a game,

Kristine Lilly

or be at one of their clinics or personal appearances. Eveywhere the players go, they are swarmed by young fans. After most games, it's common to see fans lining up by the hundreds, shouting players' names and trying to scoop up every autograph possible.

The players do everything they can to accommodate their fans. From Mia Hamm at one end of the field, to goalkeeper Briana Scurry at the other, the U.S. women take their role as soccer ambassadors very seriously.

"It's the best compliment in the world when girls come up to us and say, 'Can I have your autograph?' and, 'One day I want to play with you,'" says Shannon MacMillan, a forward/midfielder. "A lot of us never had female role models when we were growing up, let alone female soccer player role models. If we can be that for the kids who are playing today, it's only going to be great for the sport."

Julie Foudy

One youngster who especially admired U.S. co-captain Julie Foudy sent her an e-mail. *I hope this is Julie Foudy the soccer player*, the girl wrote. *You are my hero. Finally I have a role model. If it wasn't for you, I'd probably have to play golf. I hate golf.*

That girl has plenty of company. With the National Team leading the charge, women's soccer is booming throughout the United States. There are more than 7,000,000 women and girls playing, making it the most popular female team sport in the country. At the college level, women's teams actually outnumber men's teams. At the 1998 NCAA women's championship game, there was a record crowd of nearly 11,000 fans, as well as a national television audience.

More and more, the U.S. players are becoming household names and faces. Mia Hamm, Kristine Lilly, and Julie Foudy are featured in national advertising campaigns. Julie made an acclaimed broadcasting debut last summer as an ESPN studio analyst for the Men's World Cup.

"It seems like every time I pick up a magazine now, I see one of my teammates in an advertisement," goalkeeper Briana Scurry says.

There are a couple of very good reasons why the team is so popular. For one thing, they win. Although competition around the world has gotten much stiffer in the last few years, the U.S. remains the premier women's team on the planet. Over the last two years, their record is 37-3-2. In 1998, they outscored their opponents 86–11.

Tisha Venturini; Michelle Akers

For another thing, the players love what they do, and it shows. They play with total unselfishness. They radiate enthusiasm and positive energy. "We were passionate about the game when we started playing, and we're still passionate about it," Julie says. "I think that's why we've been so successful."

"If you don't keep the fun alive, what's the point in playing?" says defender Joy Fawcett, a twelve-year veteran of the team.

The team also has a very special bond— and that shows, too. They love playing together. They pull for one another.

"We've been through so much together—marriages, pregnancies, boyfriends," says Kristine Lilly. "It's all the things families go through. We really care about each other."

Adds captain Carla Overbeck, "We just

time to Norway, and finished third.

Now, on American soil, the U.S. National Team is determined to bring the Cup home again. Many of the players were part of the 1996 Olympics. They can think of nothing better than to recreate the feelings they had

Team photo shoot, 1996

have a lot of great people on our team."

"Even without soccer, I'd love hanging out with these guys," Mia Hamm says.

The U.S. captured the first Women's World Cup in 1991. Four years later, in a heartbreaking upset, the U.S. lost in over-

on the night of August 1, 1996.

That was the occasion when the record crowd turned out in Sanford Stadium—and got to see the U.S. capture the Olympic gold with a 2–1 triumph over China. When time finally expired that night, the U.S. players

Pre-game warm-up, 1996 Olympic team

Joy Fawcett; Julie Foudy

hugged, cried, and rolled around on the grass in joy. The old stadium practically shook from the noise and energy of the fans' celebration. When the players returned to the field for the medal ceremony and national anthem, the fans were still there cheering, taking more flash pictures than you see at a 100 Hanson concerts.

"It was awesome," Kristine Lilly recalls. "It was the kind of moment every athlete lives for."

Mia Hamm

looked toward the top of the stadium, awestruck that it was filled for them. Nobody wanted the moment to end. "It felt like we were floating," Shannon MacMillan says.

The next big moment in women's soccer—the 1999 World Cup—is here. The U.S. National Team's ever-growing legion of fans—including millions of soccer-playing girls—are pulling for another unforgettable finish. While they're at it, they just

During the playing of "The Star-Spangled Banner," the team held hands. They sang with the same gusto with which they had played. There were tears and chills. They might dream of being the next Mia, Kristine, Carla, or Shannon, and maybe even of floating into history themselves one day.

EDITOR'S NOTE: The players featured in this book will form the core of the 1999 Women's World Cup team, as well as the team that competes in the 2000 Summer Olympic Games. However, this book was written and published several months before a final roster could be determined. Injuries, late changes, and the emergence of rising stars could effect the final team roster. Our apologies if any players were overlooked.

Michelle Akers

HT: 5-10 WT: 150

BORN: 2/1/66

HOMETOWN: ORLANDO, FL

COLLEGE: UNIVERSITY OF
CENTRAL FLORIDA

POSITION: MIDFIELDER

It is midway through the first half of the semifinals of the 1998 Goodwill Games. The U.S. is playing Denmark. Michelle Akers controls the ball, turns, and blasts a rocket from thirty-five yards out, into the upper corner of the goal.

Akers is mobbed by her teammates. Later, amazed Danish captain Lene Torp said, "We are not used to a player being able to kick the ball in from there."

There is much about Michelle Akers that is unique. One of the most explosive scorers in history, Michelle has continued to compete for the team despite suffering from a debilitating disease through most of the 1990s. It's called chronic fatigue and immune dysfunction syndrome. At times it weakened her so much she could hardly walk around the block. In the 1996 Olympics, Michelle had to take intravenous fluids after every game. "Our trainers taped me up in so many places, they joked that I was using up half the team's budget," Michelle says.

Michelle has been part of the National Team since it began in 1985. She led the U.S. to the World Championship in the first Women's World Cup in 1991. Eight years later, at age thirty-three, Michelle is the oldest player on the team—and still among the best.

In her free time, Michelle enjoys computers and communicating with fans through her website at michelleakers.com.

"It doesn't matter where I am, as long as I'm on the field."

Brandi Chastain is nothing if not determined. Her soccer career nearly ended more than ten years ago, when a series of injuries required three knee surgeries in three years. She was out of the game for two full seasons. Then, in 1993, she was left off the National Team. Two more years went by before a new coach, Tony DiCicco, invited her to try out again.

Coach DiCicco had just one request. He wanted Brandi, who had been a forward her whole life, to try defense.

Brandi's reply? "It doesn't matter where I am, as long as I'm on the field."

Ever since, Brandi has been a mainstay of the the team's back line. Though she'll turn thirty-one shortly after the 1999 Women's World Cup, she has more passion for the game than ever. She believes it has everything to do with the time she spent away from the sport.

"I think you always appreciate things more when you've had them taken away," Brandi says.

Brandi Chastain

HT: 5-7   WT: 130

BORN: 7/21/68

HOMETOWN: SAN JOSE, CA

COLLEGE: SANTA CLARA UNIVERSITY

POSITION: DEFENDER

Joy Fawcett

HT: 5-5 WT: 130 BORN: 2/8/68

HOMETOWN: HUNTINGTON BEACH, CA

COLLEGE: UNIVERSITY OF
CALIFORNIA, BERKELEY

POSITION: DEFENDER

"You have to keep the **fun** alive— if you are not enjoying it, **what's the point?**"

Joy Fawcett may be the best-known soccer mom in the country. Not because she is always ferrying her kids to games, but because she is one of the top defenders in the world—*and* the mother of two children.

It isn't easy balancing an athletic career and family life, but Joy manages just fine. When the U.S. team makes one of its frequent trips overseas, Joy is accompanied by daughters Katelyn, five, and Carli, two, and a nanny. Along with shinguards and uniforms, Joy has to remember to pack stuffed animals, books, and diapers.

Joy has been a fixture on the U.S. defense since 1987, when she made her National Team debut at age nineteen, as Joy Biefeld. She made several spectacular defensive stops in the gold-medal game in the 1996 Olympics. She also assisted on Tiffeny Milbrett's game-winning goal.

One of nine children, Joy started playing at age five, tagging along to her older brothers' games. Even with two children in tow, Joy tries to approach soccer the same way today. She plays for the sheer joy of the game.

19

"The most important thing is knowing what it is you love."

As a girl growing up in southern California, Julie Foudy had a unique ambition. She wanted to become a sportscaster. The goal became a reality in the summer of 1998 when she did commentary for ESPN, analyzing the World Cup in France.

A veteran of twelve seasons on the U.S. National Team, Julie is much more than just a midfield standout. She's a smart, ambitious young woman. In fact, after she graduated from prestigious Stanford University with a biology degree, Julie planned to become an orthopedic surgeon.

It was a hard decision, but Julie finally decided not to pursue medicine. "There are so many other things I want to do," Julie says.

Whether it's on TV or at a clinic, the outgoing Julie loves to talk. When she has a chance to meet with young soccer players, she prefers to discuss how to have fun instead of how to play soccer. "The most important thing is knowing what it is you love," Julie says. "For me, it's soccer. For you, it might be something else. The key is just to find what you love to do, and then go after it."

Julie Foudy

HT: 5-6 WT: 130

BORN: 1/23/71

HOMETOWN: MISSION VIEJO, CA

COLLEGE: STANFORD

POSITION: MIDFIELDER

JULIE FOUDY

Mia Hamm

Ht: 5-5 Wt: 125

Born: 3/17/72

Hometown: Chapel Hill, NC

College: University of North Carolina

Position: Forward

Mia Hamm is not just the most explosive offensive threat on the U.S. Team. She is the most explosive threat in the world. After Mia scored five goals in two games in the Goodwill Games last summer, coach Tony DiCicco called it a "Michael Jordan-type performance."

The coach should know. He has seen plenty of them from Mia, a four-time winner of U.S. Soccer's Athlete of the Year award. Mia went into 1999 with 102 career goals—more than any U.S. player in history. She does it with tremendous acceleration, breathtaking ball skill, and a great grasp of the game's strategy.

Without a doubt, Mia is the most recognized female soccer player in the world. Though she appreciates the acclaim, Mia is even more humble than she is gifted. She is always praising her teammates for making her look good. "This team doesn't just have incredible talent. It has incredible people," Mia says.

The child of an Air Force family, Mia moved often as a youngster, and found that playing sports made her feel good. Her mother wanted her to be a ballerina, but the tutus were put away the minute Mia discovered soccer. She loved to run and kick. Her prowess boosted her self-esteem. More than 100 goals later, that hasn't changed.

"I really enjoy playing," Mia says. "I like the way it makes me feel about myself."

"If you can ca
the only way t
is to pul

—CAPTAIN

Kristine has worn out plenty of opponents in a dozen years on the U.S. National Team. She is the Energizer bunny of women's soccer: She just keeps going.

"She can run all day," captain Carla Overbeck says.

"She is an inspiration to the whole team with her work rate," coach Tony DiCicco says.

Kristine joined the team as a skinny sixteen-year-old from Wilton, Connecticut. She made her debut in China, and it wasn't easy. "I was petrified," Kristine says. "I was like, 'Oh, my God, I can't get in there and play with these people.'" She not only played. She scored a goal.

Kristine has made more international appearances—162—than any player, male or female, in the history of U.S. soccer. Mia Hamm may be the game's most dynamic scorer, but Mia and many others consider Kristine perhaps the best all-around player in the world.

One thing is for sure:
No player is in
better shape.

"Out of everything in soccer, I learned a long time ago the one thing I could control was my fitness," Kristine says. "It's something I take pride in."

Kristine Lilly

Ht: 5-4 Wt: 125

Born: 7/22/71

Hometown: Wilton, Ct

College: University of North Carolina

Position: Midfielder

KRISTINE
LILLY

Shannon MacMillan

Ht: 5-5 Wt: 130

Born: 10/7/74

Hometown: Escondido, Ca

College: University of Portland

Position: Midfielder/Forward

In January 1996, Shannon MacMillan got the worst news of her soccer career. U.S. National Team coach Tony DiCicco cut her from the pre-Olympic roster. Her dream of playing in the Atlanta Games seemed over.

"I was a mess," Shannon says. "I was crying my head off."

Shannon returned to the University of Portland, where she met with her coach, Clive Charles. Coach Charles told her she had two choices: She could mope, or she could work so hard that DiCicco would have no choice but to change his mind.

Shannon went right to work. The result was one of the sweetest success stories in the history of the National Team. Not only did Shannon play her way onto the squad, but she scored the so-called "golden goal" in the Olympic semifinals against arch-rival Norway. It came in sudden-death overtime, on a perfect pass from co-captain Julie Foudy.

The goal put the U.S. into the gold-medal game against China.

One game later, Shannon was standing on the top of the podium with a gold medal around her neck, holding hands with her teammates, soaking up the cheers of the overflow crowd in Athens, Georgia.

"It was just the best," she says.

For as long as women play soccer,
Tiffeny Milbrett will have a distinction
no other player can claim.

She will always be the scorer of the winning goal in the first gold-medal game in Olympic history.

She doesn't take it lightly. "I can't believe it worked out like that," Tiffeny says.

Scoring goals is certainly nothing new to Tiffeny. She was tied for the team lead with three goals in the 1995 Women's World Cup in Sweden. In a record-setting career at the University of Portland, she scored 103 goals—tying her with Mia Hamm as the all-time leading scorer in NCAA Division I competition. (In 1998, National Team member Danielle Fotopoulos set the new college mark with 118 career goals.)

Blessed with great speed and a knack for being in the right spot, Tiffeny was a two-time *Parade* magazine All-American in high school. She also starred in track and basketball. In fact, her dream is to play point guard for a professional women's basketball team. "I don't know if it'll happen, but I'd like to try," Tiffeny says.

Tiffeny Milbrett

HT: 5-2 WT: 130

BORN: 10/23/72

HOMETOWN: PORTLAND, OR

COLLEGE: UNIVERSITY OF PORTLAND

POSITION: FORWARD

Carla Overbeck

HT: 5-7   WT: 125

BORN: 5/9/68

HOMETOWN: DALLAS, TX

COLLEGE: UNIVERSITY OF NORTH CAROLINA

POSITION: DEFENDER

The 1998 Goodwill Games gold-medal match had just ended. The winning team was holding a press conference. Behind U.S. captain Carla Overbeck, her one-year-old son, Jackson, was sitting happily in a backpack, gnawing on his mother's new gold medal.

"It was just another chew toy to him," Carla says with a laugh.

Carla took a year away from the team after the Olympics to have Jackson, who was born August 14, 1997. Being a mother has brought her much joy—and made her a lot busier. But it has changed little about her life on the field, where Carla remains the ironwoman of the U.S. defense.

"Not only hasn't she lost a step, she's probably playing better than ever."

—CO-CAPTAIN JULIE FOUDY

Growing up in Dallas, Texas, Carla's sports idol was the Cowboys' quarterback, Roger Staubach. There really were no female soccer stars to look up to. That has totally changed. Now there are a host of women soccer players to admire—and one of them is a mother with a baby boy who likes to gnaw on gold medals.

Cindy Parlow

HT: 5-11 WT: 145

BORN: 5/8/78

HOMETOWN: MEMPHIS, TN

COLLEGE: UNIVERSITY OF
NORTH CAROLINA

POSITION: FORWARD

When Cindy Parlow joined the U.S. National Team at age seventeen, big things were expected of her. She was, after all, nearly unstoppable in front of the goal.

"We all knew we had a national-caliber player even when she was exceptionally young," said Anson Dorrance, Cindy's coach at North Carolina.

Still, nobody could've predicted the debut Cindy enjoyed. It came against Russia on January 14, 1996, in Campinas, Brazil. In front of some of the world's most rabid fans, Cindy pumped in two goals.

Seven months later, she had an Olympic gold medal around her neck—the youngest soccer gold medalist in history.

BORN: 6/24/75

HOMETOWN: POINT PLEASANT, NJ

COLLEGE: MONMOUTH UNIVERSITY

POSITION: DEFENDER

It was December of 1996. Christie Pearce was a senior at Monmouth University, busy being the point guard on the school basketball team. One day, a fax with her name on it arrived in the athletic department office.

The fax was sent by U.S. Soccer. It was an invitation to join the team's training camp in San Diego the following month.

Christie was shocked.

"I thought my soccer career was over," she says.

Athletic success is nothing new to Christie. Perhaps the fastest player on the U.S. team, she was the first person ever to lead her high school conference in scoring in soccer, basketball, and field hockey.

Still, her greatest thrill may have come from a fax machine.

"Even now I can't believe it," Christie says.

Christie
Pearce

HT: 5-4 WT: 112

BORN: 5/5/77

HOMETOWN: SAN RAMON, CA

COLLEGE: UNIVERSITY OF
NORTH CAROLINA

POSITION: MIDFIELDER

Tiffany Roberts

When Tiffany Roberts was in second grade, her teacher asked her to make a drawing of what she wanted to be when she grew up. "I drew a picture of me standing on an Olympic podium, with three medals," Tiffany says.

If the picture did not come totally true in 1996, it came close enough. Tiffany was one of the young stars who helped capture the Olympic gold medal.

Tiffany was just nineteen during those Games, but it was no surprise to find her there. She has always been precocious. She competed in tiny-tot running races when she was just four years old. Two years later, she fell in love with soccer. She thought briefly about becoming a cheerleader, but never got close to picking up a pom-pom.

"Cheerleading was the same time as soccer, so I wasn't going to do cheerleading," Tiffany says.

Kate Sobrero is an upbeat, likeable person. But when she steps on the soccer field, watch out. Kate is aggressive. She is single-minded. She's a tough defender with a mission, eager to block shots and slide-tackle an opponent.

"That's my favorite part of the game," Kate says.

"She's very determined and courageous," says Chris Petrucelli, coach of Notre Dame, where Kate starred for four years.

Blessed with blazing speed, Kate has shown steady improvement since first being invited to the National Team camp in January 1998. But perhaps her biggest adjustment has been getting used to being teammates with players she once idolized.

"It's pretty unbelievable," Kate says, "because I went to their camps as a kid, and now I'm like, 'Hey, Mia.'"

Kate Sobrero

HT: 5-9 WT: 140 BORN: 8/23/76

HOMETOWN: BLOOMFIELD HILLS, MI

COLLEGE: NOTRE DAME

POSITION: DEFENDER

Briana Scurry

HT: 5-8 WT: 150

BORN: 9/7/71

HOMETOWN: DAYTON, MN

COLLEGE: UNIVERSITY OF MASSACHUSETTS

POSITION: GOALKEEPER

The town of Dayton, Minnesota, is not known as a hotbed of world-class soccer talent. If anything, it's much more associated with turning out hockey players than soccer players. Briana Scurry might've wound up on the ice like everybody else—if her mother hadn't intervened.

"Hockey is the one sport she wouldn't let me play," Briana says. "She thought it was too dangerous."

The U.S. National Team is grateful for that. Briana is the winningest goalkeeper in team history. She has recorded an astonishing 42 shutouts, including 12 in 1998. In five games during the 1996 Olympics, Briana allowed just three goals.

With huge hands, great reflexes, and a fingertip-to-fingertip wingspan of six-feet, three-inches, Briana is an imposing figure in the net. But her greatest attribute may be that she thrives on the pressure.

"I guess I'm a closet control freak," she says.

"I like the whole idea that the other team can't win if they can't score on me."

Tisha Venturini may be a midfielder on the soccer field, but she's a daredevil at heart. One of her favorite activities is downhill skiing. It isn't enough for her to just find a big mountain. Tisha seeks out big jumps, fresh powder, and runs nobody else has tried. Tisha explains,

"I'm a little crazy."

Tisha has put her skiing on hold for now, because she doesn't want to risk an injury that could derail her soccer career. She has started nearly every National Team game since 1992. She loved the game long before that, following her older brother and sister, who were both avid soccer players.

"I've been playing since I could walk," Tisha says.

For Tisha, the greatest thrill is just being out on the field playing. With the World Cup this summer, and the Summer Olympics in 2000, she has two huge competitions to look forward to—and two big reasons to stay off the ski slopes.

"I'm trying to be smart about things," Tisha says, laughing.

Tisha Venturini

Ht: 5-6 Wt: 125 Born: 3/3/73

Hometown: Modesto, CA

College: University of North Carolina

Position: Midfielder

Up-and-coming Stars of USA Soccer

Saskia Webber

GOALKEEPER

The 1992 NCAA Goalkeeper of the Year, Saskia brings international experience and catlike reflexes to every game. Saskia was a valued member of the 1995 U.S. Women's World Cup Team.

Lorrie Fair

DEFENDER

Named the 1998 ESPN Defender of the Year, Lorrie—while just a junior—anchored a North Carolina defense that yielded only seven goals in 26 games.

Danielle Fotopoulos

FORWARD

Danielle holds the college record for career goals with 118. She scored the winning goal for the Florida Gators in the 1998 NCAA National Championship game.

Jen Grubb

DEFENDER

A two-time captain for Notre Dame's Fighting Irish, Jen' combination of speed and power make her one of the most promising young defenders in soccer today.

Tracy Ducar

GOALKEEPER

Tracy has been a member of the U.S. National Team since 1995, appearing in 20 games thus far. She graduated Phi Beta Kappa from the University of North Carolina.

Laurie Schwoy

MIDFIELDER

A dynamic dribbler, Laurie can turn a game with a clutch goal or stunning pass. She is a three-time All American for the North Carolina Tar Heels.

Sara Whalen

DEFENDER

A three-time All American, Sara was named the 1997 Soccer America Player of the Year. She debuted with the U.S. National Team in April 1997.

And don't forget the coach...

Tony DiCicco

COACH

"This team doesn't just have
incredible talent...

It has
incredible people."

—MIA HAMM